Deep Calls Unto Deep

Answering Questions about the Prophetic

Matthew Robert Payne

To sow into Matthew's writing ministry, to request life coaching or a personal prophecy, or to contact him, please visit http://personal-prophecy-today.com.

This book was edited by Lisa Thompson. You can email her at writebylisa@gmail.com or visit her website at www.writebylisa.com.

Cover designed by akira007 at fiverr.com.

Disclaimer: The name of the person who originally asked Matthew these questions has been changed to protect her privacy.

The opinions expressed by the author are not necessarily those of Revival Waves of Glory Books & Publishing.

Published by Revival Waves of Glory Books & Publishing PO Box 596| Litchfield, Illinois 62056 USA www.revivalwavesofgloryministries.com.

Paperback: 978-1-365-85252-7

Hardcover: 978-1-365-85254-1

Table of Contents

What should you do if you think that you have been called to be a prophet/prophetess? What types of unusual situations have you faced?

No one believes that I'm called to be a prophet. Even when it's been confirmed through others, they still make light of my calling. What should I do?

What should you do if you see, hear or sense in the Spirit when others next to you don't? How should you handle it if they call you 'crazy'?

What should you do if someone does not receive a word from you, but they do receive the word when they hear the same message from someone else?

When I am trying to explain what I believe, my words are always misunderstood or misinterpreted.

How do you handle spiritual attacks related to your calling? What should you do if someone defames you because you stated you couldn't do something for them?

Have you ever felt as if no one understands your frustrations, and even if you explained yourself, they still wouldn't understand?

Dedication

Praying Medic

This book is dedicated to a fellow author and friend of mine whose pen name is Praying Medic. David, his real name, models Jesus to me and has answered many questions for me. He is one of my favorite authors, and I like to read every book he puts out. I encourage you all to check out his books on Amazon. David is a very busy man but fits in time to have a one-on-one chat on Skype with me once in a while.

I think that everyone needs someone to look up to and to admire. David not only sells more books than I do, but he has a far-reaching ministry and many friends. He has a lovely wife who is not only his best friend, but his business partner, graphic designer and first-look editor. It is a dear pleasure of mine to be his friend. I hope you can also get to know him through his books.

Acknowledgements

Greg and Jeannie

A heartfelt 'thank you' goes out to Greg and Jeannie who, as a husband and wife, both felt impressed by the Holy Spirit to fully fund the production costs for this book. They paid for the cost of the editing, the cover design and the publishing of this book after Greg asked me for a quote. It is my prayer that many people read this book and are blessed by their generous donation. If you would like to sponsor one of my books that I will be working on soon, please email me and ask how you can help.

Father God

I want to thank you for loving me, for leading me and for making me into the person that I am today. Thank you for your Son, my best friend.

Lisa Thompson

I want to thank you for polishing my words and making this book a better book. You take my simple language and make it more readable and understandable. I want to thank you for working on so many books with me. If you need editing services, you can contact Lisa at her website at www.writebylisa.com or directly via email at writebylisa@gmail.com.

Jesus Christ

Thank you for being my friend for all of my life. You have led me and trained me, and you have allowed me to write some encouraging books. You are a joy to me. You introduced me to your Father, and now, I am getting to know him better through the years. You are closer to me than any other person outside my mother.

Bill Vincent

I want to thank Bill Vincent, who produces my paperback books, my e-books and my audio books. His company, Revival Waves of Glory Books & Publishing, has shown me great favor, and without you, I would be spending a lot more money to produce books. I give you my heartfelt thanks.

The Readers

I want to thank my readers. You have motivated me to write this. I hope that you really enjoy it and that it will be just one book that you read on the prophetic. I am no expert, but I am the very best that I can be.

June Payne

I want to thank my mother for being love to me and for being an example of patience and understanding. I appreciate how she understands me and the content that I have included in this book.

A Note from the Editor

When Matthew first informed me that he was going to release this book, I was very excited. As a person with somewhat of a prophetic gifting myself, I anticipated what he had to say. And I certainly wasn't disappointed! These 14 questions are some of the most common concerns that budding and even more experienced prophets have when they begin and as they move forward in their ministry.

An aspiring prophet might go to a meeting, hear the prophet speak and listen to him or her call out words of knowledge and pray for people. They see the "glamor" of the spotlight and think that they want that life and that they can easily do what the prophet does.

What they don't see is everything that happens behind the scenes—the years of prayer, time in the Word and developing intimacy with Jesus. They don't see the sacrifices the prophet makes—the self-denial, days of fasting and giving up friendships that don't promote a godly lifestyle.

This book delves into some of these topics and much more. You, the reader, will love hearing Matthew's perspective on how to handle some of these sensitive matters as he answers each question in his trademark simple and straightforward manner. I was thrilled to edit this for Matthew and know you will enjoy reading it!

If you have any editing needs, I am happy to help you. You can find out more about me at my website at www.writebylisa.com or email me at writebylisa@gmail.com. Happy reading, and God bless you!

Lisa

Introduction

If you have used the Amazon "Look Inside" feature, you have seen the questions that will be addressed in this book in the table of contents. This book came about when a prophetess wrote to me and asked me a number of questions. I am not very good at responding to emails, so I decided to answer her questions with voice files instead. As I answered the questions, the Holy Spirit impressed upon me that the questions with my answers might become a good little short book on the prophetic, so I bore that in mind as I responded.

You might notice that sometimes my answer seems to go "off topic" and touch on other subjects not related to the question. Since I knew that this was going to be a book to help others, I sometimes felt that other subjects needed to be said to the readers, so I addressed different topics as well.

If I asked people in my Facebook prophetic group, the "Prophetic Training Group," to provide me with a list of their questions, I am sure I could write another 50 questions for this book. I have been walking in the prophetic for decades, and I have read 50 books on the subject, and I still have questions that need answers. Although I was tempted to expand on this subject, I simply made this book about Katrina and her questions, and I hope that the enclosed information that I provide might help you so that you feel a little more "normal" if you are struggling with any of these aspects about the prophetic.

Like anything worthwhile, you will first use your gift or talent, and then you will need to practice and develop that gift. I pray that you have a lot of practice in the prophetic. I also pray that this short book encourages you and stimulates you to ask a prophet other questions that are on your mind.

This book is called "Deep Calls unto Deep" simply because the questions Katrina had for me come from a deep place, so she reached out to a fellow prophet who she knew might have answers to those questions. I pray that you also find peace as you read this book.

1 - The Calling

"Dear Matthew, What should you do if you think that you have been called to be a prophet/prophetess? What types of unusual situations have you faced?"

The first thing that I want to start with regarding this short teaching in this e-book is your initial calling as a prophet. Every person likely has a different experience when it comes to their calling. I'll just explain how I was called to be a prophet and hope that it resonates with somebody.

I originally thought that God had called me to be an evangelist. At the time, I had a friend who worked overseas. He heard a man preaching when he was in Malaysia. He went up to the man and told him, "You need to come to my country to preach at my church."

The man eventually decided to come to Australia. He gave this teaching on the five-fold ministry offices and the nine gifts of the Holy Spirit.

As he was teaching on the five-fold ministry offices, he went through the roles of each office: apostle, prophet, evangelist, pastor and teacher. As he was going down the list, explaining each role in detail, I then realized that I was called to be more than an evangelist.

I realized that the prophet is called to both non-Christians and Christians. I realized that I had been primarily acting as an evangelist. However, I would now have to minister to people inside the church, too.

For the first time, I realized that I was called as a prophet. So, no one initially prophesied to me about my calling as a prophet. I just gleaned it from this apostle's teaching, so I started to move in the prophetic. I started to buy books on the prophetic and devour them.

I used to visit internet chat rooms. My user name online was "prophetic," and I talked to people and prophesied to them.

Once, this girl came on and asked me, "Are you a prophet?"

I answered that I felt that in the future I would be in the office of prophet. "Yes, I feel I'm called to be a prophet."

She replied, "That's good because I was just upstairs, and I said to my mother who was sick in the hospital, 'I need to speak to a prophet.' " Then, she proceeded to ask me a few questions.

I started a ministry where I offered prophecies online for people, and they requested a prophecy via email.

Part of that ministry was releasing people into the prophetic and praying for them to receive the prophetic gift. I prayed for about 300 people that prophesied correctly over me to test their new gift. Some of those 300 people prophesied that I was called to be a prophet.

Firstly, you should have a sense that you're called to be a prophet. Then, God will confirm your calling through various means, which might include using two or three prophetic people to prophesy that you are called to be a prophet.

One of the hardest things to come to grips with is the fact that you're called to be a prophet. Many people struggle with the question, "Am I called to be a prophet?" Sometimes, God needs to speak 10 or 20 times to a prophet to really convince them of this truth.

We don't receive our call very easily. I think the enemy of our souls doesn't want us to accept it. Therefore, many have a lot of doubt and insecurity about their calling.

If you feel that God has called you to be a prophet and if God has spoken to you personally and told you that you're a prophet, just ask the Lord for confirmation through other prophetic people.

Some people might say you're called to be a prophet to the nations or you're called to be a prophet in your country. Once you know that you're called to be a prophet, remember that it's a very long road to develop your gifting, assignment and office. This long journey takes quite a bit of time.

The first thing that you need to come to grips with before you can come into the office of prophet is that you must know and be established in your identity and calling as a prophet.

2 - Doubts of Others

"Dear Matthew, No one believes that I'm called to be a prophet. Even when it's been confirmed through others, they still make light of my calling. What should I do?"

It's one thing to be called to be a prophet and to have that confirmed by God and by other people.

But, the people that you know—those you do life with, go to church with, who have seen your ups and downs, who have seen you upset, who have seen your struggles and disappointments as you face life's challenges—might not recognize you as a prophet.

It's hard for some of those people who do life with you to recognize that you're called to be a prophet. First of all, we have to understand that the title 'prophet' is very misunderstood. It's respected, so some people look up to it as some mystical position that only the elite can achieve.

The people who know you best over the course of your life might have a hard time coming to grips with the fact that you're called to such an esteemed and high office in God.

People do not realize that a prophet is simply a friend of God, just as Abraham and King David were. First and foremost, these men were friends of God before they were anything else. David was alone with his sheep, singing praises all day and night before Samuel called him to be the King of Israel. David cultivated friendship with God as a young shepherd boy.

If God has told us that we're called to be a prophet and if other people have confirmed it and prophesied that we're called to be a prophet, that's the most important thing. That's what should matter to us.

It should not matter whether our friends or the people we do life with at church recognize that we're called to be a prophet. Jesus understood the life of a prophet. He explained that prophets are highly revered by strangers, but in their own hometown and in their own family, they are not highly esteemed or recognized as such.

Jesus said in Mark 6:4, "But Jesus said to them, 'A prophet is not without honor except in his own country, among his own relatives, and in his own house.' " As such, Jesus was very aware of this fact, and as a prophet himself, he walked out the same situation. In the next verse, he went to Nazareth at the height of his ministry, but he wasn't able to do many miracles there or heal many people because of their unbelief.

Jesus had to be speaking from personal experience when he made that statement. When you think about whether people love and respect you and recognize you as a prophet, you've got to understand that Jesus was the most powerful minister that's ever lived on earth.

Think about it. Wherever he went, outside of his own region, people flocked to hear him speak and to seek healing from him. He healed everyone that came to him in faith. He even healed people that didn't have enough faith, such as the man with the epileptic son. He was well sought after. It must have really hurt his feelings to come to his hometown with all that power and to not be able to heal people that he loved and cared about. The sting of his own hometown rejection must have deeply hurt him.

In Matthew 12:47, people came to Jesus and told him, "Your mother and your sisters and brothers are outside." Jesus answered, "Who is my mother and my sisters and my brothers? Aren't they the people that follow me and obey me?"

Jesus was saying in this passage that his family members only knew him in the flesh. His brothers only knew him as a brother. They don't know him as a Messiah. The people who recognized him as a Messiah, the anointed one, were the people that followed him. They were more like his mother and sisters and brothers. But those people out there that called themselves his mother and sisters and brothers didn't believe in him the way that those who knew him as Messiah did.

It is difficult to grow up in a church as a prophet. You might be in a situation for many years where the only people that recognize you as a prophet are those online.

Only strangers might know your gifting. Like Jesus said, a prophet is not without honor except in his own hometown and among his own family. In other words, everyone outside of his own hometown and his own family honors him.

As a result, you'll find that people who are total strangers to you respect your anointing and your call as a prophet. But those who are close to you don't really understand you and your calling.

Of course, people make light of the situation. One of the reasons that your friends and others don't recognize you as a prophet is because if they did, they would have to listen to what you have to say. This recognition comes with a sense of accountability that comes into play when they recognize that you're a prophet.

Once they acknowledge your prophetic ability and if you have told them about your revelations or what God has told you to do or the direction you believe they should go, then they will need to accept your words if they recognize your office.

People don't like to accept that you're a prophet just as an atheist doesn't accept that there is a God. If he accepted that there was a God, he would have to be accountable to that God. One of the main reasons that they might not recognize you is because of that accountability.

It might take you many years to find a church that recognizes your gift and your office. In fact, you might never find a church that accepts your office, but that does not mean that you remove yourself from fellowship. Jesus didn't remove himself forever from his own hometown, but he went to where people accepted him and his ministry.

It took me many years to come to grips with this. I spent a long time wondering why my pastors would not invite me to speak at my church. I remember weeping many times over this issue. Jesus spoke to me and told me that he said that a prophet is not without honor except in his own hometown and family, similar to my situation. He told me that this verse was put in the Bible by the Holy Spirit to address the hurt in my heart.

With this book, I have now written 26 books. I have between 500 and 800 people buy a book from me every month. Many strangers are learning from me. I have met people on Facebook who have written to me who tell me that I am one of their favorite teachers. I have met people online that have read all my books. I calculated that it would take about 60 hours to read all of them. This person who has all my books will invest 60 hours of their time in listening to me, but people in my own church won't let me speak for 20 minutes.

Do you know that if Jesus hadn't risen from the dead, James, his eldest brother under him, would have never committed his life as a Christian? Did you know that Jesus could not convince his own brother of the faith he possessed?

After 3 and a half years of walking with Jesus, Peter, one of the three disciples in Jesus' inner circle, still didn't understand that one of the purposes of Jesus on earth was to die for the sins of the world. He had told his disciples many times that he was going to die and rise again, but even his closest disciples didn't understand his mission.

And so it is with us. The people that love us the most can't see us or understand us. I have a friend on Facebook that has given me $1,500, which is a lot of money, to publish this book. Yet, none of the people that I know locally have ever ordered a paperback book of mine, which would cost them about $35 to be shipped to Australia.

I want you to understand this point, dear reader. People who know you the best simply won't understand the call on your life. If you are called to be a prophet, you will be blessed to have a friend that you can speak with over coffee for hours with about the deep things of the Lord. I do not have these types of friends who live near me although I do have friends that are oversees that I can Skype with for hours.

MATTHEW ROBERT PAYNE

3 - Seeing when Others Don't

"Dear Matthew, What should you do if you see, hear or sense in the Spirit when others next to you don't? How should you handle it if they call you 'crazy'?"

I am very open to the supernatural, which is discernment of spirits. I see and recognize things that others don't pick up on.

For instance, I might wonder about a certain direction to take in life regarding a decision that I need to make. I might see a sign on the street that says "Wrong way, go back."

A person traveling in the car with me might not recognize that this sign is telling me prophetically to change direction. A random sign might change the total course of my life.

A person might actually think you're crazy if you decided to go one way with the Lord and then suddenly changed your mind just because of a street sign.

If the person with you saw the sign and if you can explain to them that the sign was speaking to you spiritually and telling you that your decision to pursue this matter was wrong and that God was changing your mind, the person might think that you're absolutely crazy.

Many times, I am walking down the street, and I'll see a sign on a billboard or an advertisement at a bus stop with a message for me. One of the signs might say, "pure genius," which is the Lord telling me, "Matthew, you're a pure genius."

Most people don't understand the ideas and plans of a genius or what he or she says. They only recognize the invention or the creation of the genius after the fact. Many geniuses are lonely until they've created and designed their invention and gotten it up and running. Others don't really understand their ideas or what they're up to. And no one really understands them.

If I'm walking down the street with someone, and I see a sign that says, "pure genius," that person might see the same sign and recognize the product that it's advertising and think that it's a genius product. They only see the sign in the natural while I see it as prophetic.

However, they won't receive the same message that God was speaking to me that I'm a pure genius. I gave my first novel to an English teacher to edit and proofread. She told me that when she finished editing it that the way that I developed the characters and weaved the characters throughout the story was the work of a pure genius. She and others have called me a genius. This is a character trait that has been highlighted in my life.

When I saw the sign that said, "pure genius," it resonated with me that God was talking about me. Now, that advertisement has a person who created it. The creator of the ad had no idea that their marketing campaign would speak to me.

You might not be wired like me. None of this might make any sense to you. But a person with a high degree of discerning of spirits will understand what I am talking about.

In other situations, I've seen a whole group of angels, and before I realized what I was doing, I actually asked someone, "Can you see these angels?" The person I asked, who does not have spiritual eyes, thinks they are with someone that is absolutely stark, raving mad.

Over time, I have learned to recognize what I'm seeing and what others are seeing. I know now to mostly keep my mouth shut when it comes to visions and the angelic. I also know when a song on the radio or an advertising sign has a message for me, but I keep those messages to myself.

In the past, I have prayed for people as I've been led by the Holy Spirit to open their spiritual eyes. I pointed out people in the vision to them, and they've been able to see the saints or angels and experience the same vision that I was seeing.

This comes down to having the wisdom to be able to discern if you are with a person that can comprehend what you're sensing in the Spirit. Is the person as spiritually in tune as you are?

Most of the time, the average Christian who attends church on Sunday and reads their Bible from time to time will not really know much about the supernatural. That person might not live an on-fire spiritual or supernatural life.

This is sad. Most of the time, we're experiencing supernatural phenomena. We should usually keep our mouths shut, or the few friends that we do have will distance themselves from us. They won't understand when we talk about things that don't make sense to them.

To find out more about the gift of discernment of spirits and to help you understand yourself better, I highly recommend these two YouTube videos, both Part 1 and Part 2.

First, I will tell you the titles to search under if you are reading the paperback, and second, I will give you the YouTube links if you are on a Kindle.

Jennifer Eivaz - Part 1: The Gift of Discerning of Spirits[1]

https://www.youtube.com/watch?v=2kgZtjFLPbk

Part 2: The Gift of Discerning of Spirits[2]

https://www.youtube.com/watch?v=eR65Dw3mrCo

---

[1] Link accessed and active as of Feb. 7, 2017.
[2] Link accessed and active as of Feb. 7, 2017.

MATTHEW ROBERT PAYNE

4 - The Response of People

"Dear Matthew, When sharing God's message with his people, they often reject what I say. However, when they hear the same message from someone else, they receive it. How should I handle this? It's very discouraging."

This answer comes down to if people really receive you as an authority in their lives. If they don't recognize you as a prophet or as someone who knows God and has a strong relationship with him and if they don't understand who you are and don't recognize your authority in the Kingdom of God, what you say to them probably won't be taken seriously.

People don't really pay attention to what you have to say if they don't recognize your office. You might tell them that there's no pre-tribulation rapture and that people will go through the tribulation. You might tell them that Jesus will come much later, and the whole idea of the rapture doesn't make sense, but they won't pay attention to you.

For many years, I told that to my parents. They simply didn't believe me. Instead, they believed the man on TV that was preaching in front of 5,000 people at his church when he talked about the rapture. They believed him because he had a stage with 5,000 people in the audience.

He has authority and is on TV. Of course, they think he's right. He can afford to broadcast his programs on TV. I am just their son. All I am is someone who previously had a mental illness and who was unstable in the past. For that reason, they assume that not everything I hear is from God.

They think that because I was deceived in the past that I am still deceived when it comes to what I say about the rapture and what I say about when Jesus is actually coming for his Bride.

Of course, the same parents can listen to someone else on TV, and they can share reasons why the rapture won't happen before the tribulation, but that it will happen later. The person on TV is making the very same arguments, using the same Scriptures that I use. I see my parents receive what that person says but not receive what I say.

This comes back to the fact that a prophet is not without honor except in his own hometown and among his own family. Readers, this is because these people know you and call themselves personal friends of yours.

In other words, they don't respect you in the office of prophet, and they don't respect the revelations that you have about Scripture.

As a prophet, you read the Bible and see things very deeply. As a prophet myself, just half a page of the Bible fills me up with revelation, and I can't even read a full page of the Bible because it's so full of life and revelation that I just can't process it all.

As a prophet, you see deeply into the Bible. Since you're a friend of the Lord's, he speaks to you and gives you revelations. However, the revelations that you actually receive from the Lord might not help your friends or those that you know from church because they know you, and they're part of the group in your own hometown that Jesus was talking about.

They don't revere you as a prophet, so they don't respect your words. Therefore, you can say the same words and information as someone else, such as a message, a revelation or a teaching from the Bible to your friends and acquaintances, and they might just look at you with a blank stare and not receive what you're saying or do what you suggest.

Yet, someone else can come along, such as a guest speaker at your church who shares the same revelation with your friends, and suddenly they are talking to you about the revelation and sharing how profound and amazing the revelation was.

You can save your breath, but you can hear yourself saying to them, "Two years ago, I told you the same thing." No matter how many times you tell people something, they don't receive it if they are from your hometown. They don't accept it because they're familiar with you.

That's one of the hardest parts of the calling on your life as a prophet. People that know you, that do life with you, that associate with you, will not receive from or respect or honor you. You have no authority in their life.

You might struggle to come to grips with the fact that those in your hometown won't receive you. However, Jesus made these statements for a reason. Remember, he was a prophet in his own hometown but wasn't received there. His family treated him as flesh and blood and didn't respect him and honor him as a prophet.

If you've received revelations and teachings for your friends, they might not receive them. Over time, you become more experienced and more knowledgeable and understand these principles. You stop sharing your revelation with your friends because you realize that you are wasting your breath and wasting your time and theirs.

You might become a writer and start to write ideas and concepts for total strangers who will receive you as a prophet and listen to what you have to say.

In closing, I have also shared something with a man who was blown away by the revelation. He told his wife how profound it was, and the wife became upset, saying, "I have been telling you that for years!" I have to confess that this happened when I was new to a church, and I was a "stranger" to the people.

5 - Often Misunderstood

"Dear Matthew, When I am trying to explain what I believe, my words are always misunderstood or misinterpreted."

This is very common, and it's hard to get around and hard to change. You are coming from a certain perspective and coming from a depth of relationship with Jesus Christ and a maturity in him and knowledge of the Word. When you're coming from a place that is distinct and precious to God, you can share things that you feel are elementary and simple with people, and they might not understand what you're actually talking about.

For example, some Bible teachers are hard to understand. Their content is so deep that you need to pay very close attention to grasp the meaning. Others agree and say that they have listened to the message many times before they finally understand what the teacher said.

That's not what I mean, and it's not what Katrina means, either. However, this helps me make my point. Just as I find what these aforementioned teachers say is hard to understand, the nominal Christian, the person who simply goes to church and doesn't really put any effort into their Christian faith and who is not called to ministry and who does not have a deep relationship with Jesus Christ, finds things that I say too hard to understand.

These people don't understand things that seem elementary to us. However, we walk in the Spirit and in the presence of Jesus all day and fellowship and minister with the Spirit throughout each day. This opens our understanding to the things of God.

We should be directed by the Holy Spirit each day. Although these matters seem fairly simple to me, others feel they are complex and misunderstand them. They can't comprehend what it is even like to be led by the Holy Spirit.

They don't understand that the Holy Spirit can plan each of your steps and guide your day and direct you, taking away even the need for you to make decisions about your life because the Holy Spirit helps you make all those decisions.

While this seems pretty simple and fundamental to me and is just how I live my life as led by the Holy Spirit, others misunderstand and misinterpret this if I try and share it with them.

As a prophet, you see really deeply into the Bible and have a lot of revelation from the Scriptures. You are not like the average person who reads the Bible and becomes bored.

Reading the Bible was boring for me in the past. The average Christian can read pages of God's Word when it doesn't jump out at them, and they get little if anything from it.

However, just half a page of the Bible contains a tremendous amount of downloads for me. It's almost too much for me to absorb. This is because I am a deep person and because I've got a great relationship with the living Word of God, Jesus, so his Word really resonates with me.

Sadly, you can explain things that you feel are easy to understand to people because you're living on a different plane and because you have a higher frequency of relationship with Jesus. What seems plain to you is misunderstood and misinterpreted by other people.

Paul spoke about this dilemma we face in 1 Corinthians 2:9-16, "But as it is written: "Eye has not seen, nor ear heard, Nor have entered into the heart of man The things which God has prepared for those who love Him.""

"But God has revealed them to us through His Spirit. For the Spirit searches all things, yes, the deep things of God. For what man knows the things of a man except the spirit of the man which is in him? Even so no one knows the things of God except the Spirit of God. Now we have received, not the spirit of the world, but the Spirit who is from God, that we might know the things that have been freely given to us by God.

"These things we also speak, not in words which man's wisdom teaches but which the Holy Spirit teaches, comparing spiritual things with spiritual. But the natural man does not receive the things of the Spirit of God, for they are foolishness to him; nor can he know *them,* because they are spiritually discerned. But he who is spiritual judges all things, yet he himself is *rightly* judged by no one. For "who has known the mind of the Lord that he may instruct Him?" But we have the mind of Christ."

I have often shared a revelation with a person about what Jesus was showing me in the Bible. However, my words made no sense to them, and they looked at me like I was crazy or even stupid. They simply misunderstand and misinterpret my words.

You might turn off some people immediately at this point. When we share revelation of the Holy Spirit with a person, he or she might have no internal grid for it. What you are sharing might go against popular doctrine or church traditions, and because the person hasn't received the same revelation, they conclude that you are wrong or even a heretic.

I came to a point where I didn't usually share things with people because I was sick and tired of people giving me strange looks or thinking that I was crazy.

I'm fortunate to have people who read my books and that God inspires me to write books and share my wisdom with strangers who download my books. I have a willing audience of people to listen to me, who want to listen to me, who want to learn from me and who want to grow in their relationship with Jesus Christ. Many people who read one of my books go on to read another one or more or even all of my books. The people that really love my relationship with the Lord and that love the way that I write come back time and time again to read more of my books.

Through writing books and blogs, I have an open audience to speak to, which diminishes my need to share revelations with people that I go to church with since the average Christian simply can't understand the same truths that I understand and walk in.

This is similar to the speaker I mentioned who is very hard for me to understand. The same is true for us when we're speaking to an average Christian. We're on another level, on another frequency. What we say is misinterpreted and misunderstood by other people because we're coming from another perspective.

Even when we try to make it simple and plain, they don't have the hundreds of hours of prayer and foundation with the Lord and experience to be able to sift through and understand what we have to say.

If you are reading this book, and you are not called to be a prophet, I might seem really harsh in my assessment of other Christians. If you look at the list of my books, you will see that I have three other books on the prophetic, yet most of my books are written to address the average Christian and to lift them up higher. My life's purpose is to raise people to another level and have them join me where I am. However, since most people reading this book are called to be prophets, my tone toward others might seem demeaning. I apologize for that.

6 - Spiritual Attacks

"Dear Matthew, How do you handle spiritual attacks related to your calling? What should you do if someone defames you because you stated you couldn't do something for them?"

I don't know what it is about people. Others are attracted to us, but they only want us to use us for their benefit.

When you lack friends, which is the case with many prophets, you might find yourself compromising and accepting others so that you have someone to talk to. Some of these individuals might use you.

When you're known as a prophet, you have many people write to you. When they discover that you're a prophet, they might ask for a free prophecy. For many years, I gave free prophecies to anyone who asked. In fact, I still run a Facebook group where I give free prophecies to people.

I didn't mind people writing and requesting a prophecy, so I would send them a word. However, after this happened repeatedly, I became burned out.

Satan allowed me to burn out from all the prophecies that I gave. I became sick and tired of people writing to me. They didn't even know me but just friended me on Facebook when they found out that I'm a prophet. They might have read one of my books or somehow found out about me. These people wrote to me, asking for a prophecy.

I wrote back to a lot of them and told them that I don't do prophecies for strangers any more. Many of them have responded abusively, calling me a false prophet or other rude names.

Yes, I understand your question about attacks, criticisms and rumors. They say things about you that are not true simply because you refused to do something for them for free that they wanted, that they thought was important. They assumed that you would just give them a prophecy.

However, if you have strong boundaries in place, you probably will not continually prophesy over random strangers who ask you for words. Your boundaries upset people when they learn that they can't use and abuse you.

Prophets especially need to watch out for those with a Jezebel spirit as they will suck the life out of you. Many of the people that want something from you and that are very demanding have a Jezebel spirit.

However, I struggle when it comes to discerning a Jezebel spirit in someone. The first indication that I usually have that the person has a Jezebel spirit is when they thrust a spiritual knife through me.

The Jezebel spirit has insulted me, said something negative with spiritual ramifications or hurt me really badly. When someone has attacked me with a spiritual knife, it really wounds me. I then have a check in my spirit that this person is attacking me with a wrong spirit.

I don't have many friends. As I'm writing this book and sharing these things with Katrina, I haven't been to church for about 10 weeks. In a way, I'm happy not going to church at the moment. I do go to a group called Toastmasters, a public speaking organization, where I meet people and associate with friends.

Aside from Toastmasters and my friends on the Internet, I really don't have many friends. I do know people at church, but I haven't connected with any of them since I have been gone for the past 10 weeks. I really can't be sure that I have many friends.

When you don't have many friends, you will more easily accept people into your life with a wrong spirit. Soon enough, when you don't do something for these people with a controlling Jezebel spirit, they will go out of their way to speak negatively to other people and defame you.

Those with a controlling Jezebel spirit want things their way; they want you to do things for them. If you don't march to their orders and bow to their demands, then they feel obligated to warn off people and tell others about how you're not doing what they want you to do.

Of course, they don't explain the whole situation to others or tell them how demanding they have been and that you have simply set appropriate boundaries with them. Instead, they complain that you are not being reasonable. They gossip about you and act like they are right, acting like you're not really a prophet because if you were, you'd help them and do what they want you to do.

As such, they cleverly manipulate the situation, trying to defame you and cut you down to others.

When you make an enemy of a Jezebel, they go out of their way to destroy you and take your friends by attacking you.

People with the Jezebel spirit actually hate prophets. However, very few people with a Jezebel spirit have any idea that they actually have that spirit. If you confronted them, they would completely deny it.

I am not saying here that anyone who makes demands of you as a prophet has the Jezebel spirit. Many strangers write to me and ask for a personal prophecy. When I tell them that I only give prophecies for a donation now and then send them my website, many of them fire back insults at me and claim that I am a false prophet. I still don't understand their logic. If I agreed to give them a prophecy, they would receive it and believe that God was speaking to them. But when I say that I won't prophesy over them, they immediately claim that I am a false prophet.

I know that if you are called to be a prophet, you will have people with the Jezebel spirit come against you. To better discern people that might have that spirit, you might want to learn more about it. Bill Vincent, my publisher, has written an excellent book on the subject available through Amazon called, "Destroying the Jezebel Spirit: How to Overcome the Spirit Before It Destroys You!"

MATTHEW ROBERT PAYNE

7 - Isolation

"Dear Matthew, What should you do when you feel alone and isolated because your friends stopped talking to you? Do you just talk to God more? Do you have other advice?"

At this stage in my Christian walk, I don't have many friends. People at church like me, but I've been away from church for 10 weeks now, and none of them have contacted me.

I've been through times in my life where I've been friendless. Sometimes as a prophet, your friends stop talking to you. I think this happens when you become closer to God. The closer you become to God, the more spiritually minded and the less carnal you become, and the less you have in common with your friends.

You become interested in God's Kingdom, God's works, God's desires and God's will in your life. Other people are interested in handbags, new clothes, TV and sporting events. You're interested in the plans and thoughts of God. They're interested in their friends, in what's trending on Facebook and in what exciting and new series has come to TV.

You're interested in advancing the Kingdom while they're interested in advancing their positions and their knowledge of what's popular in the world.

Thomas Kempis in his book, "The Imitation of Christ," said that when you're really close to God, you won't have any friends.[3]

I was particularly impressed by that because at the time, I only had one friend locally. Now, I have friends on Facebook, but I really don't have friends in my city. I talk to people at Toastmasters, but I don't see them outside of the group.

I consider a friend someone that you see outside of where you see them regularly. I consider a person from church my friend if I saw them outside of church. If I only see them at church, then I don't really consider them my friends.

I have felt isolated. I'm now used to keeping myself busy and entertained. I usually call my mom a couple of times a day to talk with her.

---

[3] https://www.christianbook.com/the-imitation-christ-book-and-mp3/thomas-kempis/9781598566864/pd/566864?dv=c&en=google&event=SHOP&kw=christian-living-0-20%7C566864&p=1179710&gclid=CjwKEAiArvTFBRCLq5-7-MSJ0jMSJABHBvp05plZtmhk5DEau1oVBOCybgZiUvkmihzUO2r6sjSncxoCQnbw_wcB

It's hard not to feel sad or lonely. Even so, this really helps you develop a deeper and deeper relationship with the Lord. Deep really does call to deep.

People might balk at this and think I'm crazy, but Jesus, as well as saints from heaven, visit me. People from the Bible come down and spend time with me. A number of them visit me on earth. They're the great cloud of witnesses mentioned in Hebrews 12:1. They are friends of mine, and they understand me like God understands me. I have good relationships with them.

I'm a friendly person who encourages others and brings joy to them. At the same time, I'm very deep and serious. I'm focused and intentional about God's business and his will for my life.

Many Christians wear God like an accessory, like a woman carries her handbag. Of course, a handbag is important to a woman, but she can leave it on a table until she goes out again. She might even exchange that handbag for another one, depending on what she's wearing.

Like the handbag, God can conveniently be carried around. But he's not essential to the person as he can be picked up and put down again.

Jesus is everything to me. He is the reason I live. He gives me directions each day. Every week and every month, I'm working on another book. Every day, I check on how many people have my books. Every day, I oversee Facebook groups and minister to other people.

My whole life is focused around God and his Kingdom and what he's doing in me. I want to help people come to grips with who they are and find their destiny and start to walk in their calling.

I give prophetic words to people that write to my ministry and request a prophecy for $30 Australian dollars. People who value the prophetic don't mind paying $30 for a word.

Half of the people that request a prophetic word give me great feedback and share that they were touched by the prophetic words. My days generally consist of giving prophecies, writing books and pursuing Jesus.

I am closer to Jesus than most other Christians are. He's a very close friend of mine. God is very close to me also. We have great fellowship. I know the mind of God. I have the heart of God and of Jesus; his love flows through me.

I can easily connect with strangers and give them prophetic words. Since I'm lonely and don't have many friends, I'm really outgoing and pleasant to strangers and people that serve me in shops. I make friends with the people that I see in the community, such as grocery store cashiers.

I interact well with strangers when I'm eating and doing business and going places. The strangers that meet me are blessed. A couple of people in local shops have become my friends. I interact with them and with my mother.

Whenever I write a book, I treat the people that are reading it as my friends. I speak to them openly and willingly share my heart with them.

If God loves us and wants us for himself as prophets, it must be good for us to be alone.

8 - Balancing Home and Ministry

"Dear Matthew, What should you do if your spouse becomes upset or jealous because you are at church or gone a lot for ministry? How should you handle it if your spouse wants you with him or her all the time because you carry the presence of God?"

First of all, I don't have a spouse, so it's hard for me to specifically answer this question for you. Even so, I can understand your question. You're essentially asking if my spouse was ever upset or jealous because of the presence of God that was with me.

Yes, a spouse will grow used to the presence of God because his Spirit resides in you. When you leave or when you go to church, they can become upset because the peace and the presence of God has departed from the house.

When Jesus sent his disciples out, he told them, "If the household is worthy, let your peace come upon it. But if it is not worthy, let your peace return to you" (Matthew 10:13).

This verse shows that the presence and the peace of God actually travel with people. Your presence in the house can bring the presence of God. So one thing that I take from this question is that your spouse isn't as spiritual as you are because if he were, he'd carry the presence of God as well. In that way, he wouldn't miss the presence of the Lord when you left.

Your spouse doesn't seem to be as close to the Lord as you are. The presence of God takes a while to manifest in a person's life. I'd love to write on the presence of God and share about this subject with people. I know the presence of God consists of love, joy and peace.

I know that in the presence of God is plenty of joy and plenty of peace. I was visiting my mother's house once. She told me that I was very peaceful, that when I was staying with them, a lot of peace was in the house. She was talking about the presence of God, and I was really happy to know that she'd noticed the shift, the change in the atmosphere because I was there.

This is similar to what you're talking about. The peace of God resides in you, and your spouse actually becomes upset, saddened and frustrated with the fact that peace leaves the house when you leave.

However, you can't help another person become closer to God. You can share a book with them or ideas and keys on how to grow closer to God, but the person has to go through the actual process for themselves.

You can't just give them a book or just pray a prayer over them so that they are instantly changed and closer to God with a more established relationship with him.

A person has to spend time in the presence of God. They have to draw close to God for themselves so that they can have a dynamic relationship with him.

I can understand that people out there have relationships where they are the more spiritual one of the couple. In some cases, couples have an imbalance in the relationship that each of you has with God.

It's sad but true that in many relationships, one person seems to be closer to God, and the other person seems to be lacking. I don't hear of many relationships where both partners are very close to God and pressing into him with passion.

Many times, one of them is lacking in their relationship with God. I can pray for your spouse that he would draw closer to God. I'll pray that he'd start to recognize that the presence of God is with you and that he will develop his own relationship with God so that God's presence resides with him. In that way, he won't depend on you all the time for the home to feel peaceful.

I pray that you'll be able to cope with his bad moods and with his upset emotions. Husbands might try to stop their wives from going to church simply because of that fact that they don't want to miss the peace and the presence of God while their wife is away at church.

Both wives and husbands might not be allowed to go to church because of that. We can thank God that this isn't happening to you at the moment, and I pray that this will never happen to you. But I feel badly for anyone who is experiencing this.

Amazing peace and joy is found in the presence of God. The Holy Spirit likes to dwell with and inhabit people who honor Jesus, who love and follow him with all their heart. He likes to reside in and spend time with those people and communicate and walk with them.

When the Holy Spirit comes and rests on you and makes his habitation with you, then you experience peace and joy and his direction in all that you think and all that you do.

Enjoying his presence is a tremendously wonderful experience, and I would highly miss it if the presence departed from me.

I've had times of past depression where the presence has basically left me. But thankfully, I've been prayed for and delivered, and I haven't suffered from depression in six months.

I hope that answers your question. I hope that you feel that I understand where you're at, and I pray that your relationship will improve.

MATTHEW ROBERT PAYNE

9 - Challenging Situations

"Dear Matthew, How do you handle it if you feel like you are going through hell on earth? What if others don't understand because they haven't suffered like you have?"

That's an amazing question, and I have quite a bit to say about this. I have to say first of all, that I question your wording when you say, "Have you ever felt like you're living in pure hell on earth?" I don't know if I would use those words because I've visited hell before, and it's a very scary place. Even so, I understand what you mean.

Life on earth seems to have been a place of unbearable suffering for you. When others haven't suffered like you or if they haven't experienced some of the dreadful situations you've faced, life seems even harder. People don't understand and can't relate to you.

Sometimes, people don't have a grid to understand us. They have no idea where you're coming from. I've lived a difficult life and gone through some suffering on earth that has been really tragic and trying. I've been pushed to my limit. I still go through struggles and trials with certain sins and temptations in my life that resurface from time to time and cause me grief.

I understand suffering, and I understand those who have gone through hard times. I think you have a real advantage when you have endured much and gone through unbearable trauma on earth. You become a very good listener, and you have a lot of compassion built into you so that you understand people's struggles. As you go through suffering yourself, you develop a capacity to understand others. This compassion is forged through your own trials—to listen to people and to be able to understand the hardships that they're going through.

I can relate to the fact that people simply don't understand you. If you have decided to try and explain the suffering that you've been through, some people will cut you off and tell you that they don't want to hear about your problems or tell you that you're dredging up the past. They might tell you that it is not helpful to discuss the past and that no one will benefit from it. They might not want to hear such dreadful things.

They will say, "It's not edifying or positive. We should be talking about the future; we shouldn't be talking about the sufferings you've been through. You need to get on with your life and get over it and face today. Tomorrow is a new day, and you should just be positive. You shouldn't be dwelling on those things of the past."

They will have all sorts of excuses. They have all sorts of platitudes to quickly dismiss the sufferings that you've been through and shut you down so that you quit talking about your hard times.

By and large, people are not very interested in sufferings. They don't want to hear about your problems or the difficulties that you've been through. Most people only want to hear the positive and the blessings. They want to hear about increasing their wealth, possessions and happiness.

They don't want to dwell on hardships, trials or struggles that you've been through because it's not encouraging or uplifting. They don't think it's of any benefit. People are dismissive of your problems and really don't pay attention or even try to understand what we've been through.

I've wrote about my pain in my book "His Redeeming Love - a Memoir." In that book, I poured out my heart and told a really graphic story of my past and the life I've lived. I've found that out of my 26 books, that book sold the third least number of copies. Not many people buy that book, which proves that people want to know about things that are going to benefit, increase and prosper them. They're not interested in hearing the sad stories of a prophet or of a prophet's struggles.

I understand that life on earth can be difficult. I used to say that I don't like going to heaven because I don't like returning to earth. It's so depressing to come back to earth.

About 700 people a month now read my books on Kindle. I know that I'm affecting 700 people a month, which helps me enjoy life because I know that I'm making a difference. But if I weren't making any noticeable difference here, life on earth would be really tough. If I were experiencing a lack of friendship and lack of direction and lack of purpose here, earth would be like a living hell to me.

I understand if you're not achieving much in the prophetic or if you're not being used by God very effectively at the moment, it would affect and hurt you. I understand that life on earth can be very difficult. It takes some time to reach a stage in your prophetic walk where you're actually being used by God. Eventually, you reach a point where you're happy to be alive and to be on this earth.

It takes a while to reach a place where you're blessing to others, and you start to actually enjoy your life and what you do. I'm in a season where life is tough for me, but I know that I'm making a difference to people just like you. You might have begun by reading my book, "A Beginner's Guide to the Prophetic." I know that I've touched your life and through these recordings and this eventual book, I'll touch many others.

10 - Dealing with People

"Dear Matthew, Here is my current situation. Have you ever felt like your solace is in God alone? You sense when people are in their flesh, which really irritates you."

This is a very interesting subject. Part of the life and the call of the prophet is to be God's friend. The history of the Bible tells the stories of people who are friends of God, and they're not really understood by others. Elijah and King David are prime examples.

Jeremiah is another example. People didn't believe him, yet he had a vital and relevant message for his world. Most of the prophets in the Bible were killed by the very people that they were called to share God's messages with. Thankfully, today, prophets are not usually killed. Even so, I look at people like David and Solomon, and I praise God for what they wrote.

The people in the Bible who were friends of God didn't seem to have other friends that really understood them. David continually poured out his heart to God, sharing that he was being attacked on all sides and that his enemies were after him. He cried on his pillow all night long, and he actually writes about it and tells us of his sorrow.

David had a few wives, but they did not even seem to be there for him when he needed love, attention and understanding. Part of the role of a prophet is to be set apart, to be holy and consecrated to the Lord. This means living for God and his will and his purposes in your life. Like I said before, being led by the Holy Spirit means that you allow him to decide what you will do. Being set apart means that you let him make your decisions for you.

I didn't know what I was going to do today. I opened your email and read the questions there. You seemed to have so many questions, and so much could be said about each one. I decided to answer them by making audio files and sending them to you. When I decided to create the files, the Holy Spirit impressed upon me that I could make each one into chapters in a book. I could write a short book with the answers to your questions. That is just one example of being led by the Spirit.

Other people, including your friends, might think it's strange for you to be able to make decisions and receive directions from God so that your whole life is directed by him. Many Christians don't understand what it's like to be led and directed by the Holy Spirit, so they live in the flesh as you said. They don't know God or find solace in him. As you said, when people live in the flesh, it's irritating.

I can understand how you feel. These people only know how to live in the flesh. They've never taken the time to press into God or to draw close to him. They have no grid for living and being led by the Holy Spirit.

They don't know what the presence of God is besides worship time at church. The only time they enter the presence and peace and joy of the Lord is during praise and worship. However, they don't walk in that presence during the week. They're not directed by the Holy Spirit. Their life is carnal. They concentrate on possessions and TV shows and good reputations and appearances and keeping up with the Jones'.

Sadly, they're not concerned about the Kingdom of God or about God's will or about being directed by him. Because of all that, they have a fleshly and carnal life.

They're supposed to be Christians, led by God, and they're supposed to find a meaningful life in God, but they're far removed from him. That's why it's up to us as prophets to encourage the average Christian to draw close to God, to teach the average Christians the following:

- How to find their purpose
- How to find direction
- How to walk in the Holy Spirit
- How to be directed by God and

- How to pursue the will of God for their life.

I have written and published a book called "Finding your Purpose in Christ" that gives you more information about each of these topics. I hope that many people buy that book and learn to find their purpose and to walk in it.

As prophets, we are meant to teach the average Christian the following:

- How to hear God speak
- How to listen to him
- How to walk in the Spirit and
- How to do many other spiritual things.

Our job is to direct the carnal people into a life that's spiritual, into the kind of life we live. Part of the prophet's job isn't necessarily to prophesy to people but to teach them how to walk like we do, how to live like we do, how to be satisfied with life like we are and how to be fulfilled in life like we are.

Many people have their focus on the world and the things of the world, so the world attracts them. They are addicted to the things and the pleasures of the world.

1 John 2:15-17 talks about this as follows:

"Do not love this world nor the things it offers you, for when you love the world, you do not have the love of the Father in you. For the world offers only a craving for physical pleasure, a craving for everything we see, and pride in our achievements and possessions. These are not from the Father, but are from this world. And this world is fading away, along with everything that people crave. But anyone who does what pleases God will live forever."

People need to learn how to divorce themselves from the affairs of the world and the things of the world. These people aren't the right people to direct them to the better way of living.

Like I said, our friends often don't respect or honor us as prophets, so they won't really listen to us or be directed by us. They likely won't respond well to a book that we have written. Instead, we need to read a book from someone else about how to live in the Spirit, how to be directed by the Spirit or how to hear from God. We need to give them a copy of that book and hope that they read it and apply it to their life.

I will add this final note that I did not include in the recordings. When you live a life that is set apart and focused wholly on God and his will for your life, you might feel frustrated to hear people talk about things of no consequence that really don't matter. However, to maintain friendships and relationships, you have to expect some give and take.

I am sure that Jesus was not always talking about profound subjects. I am sure that he spoke to a lady who cooked a meal that he ate and told her that he enjoyed the meal. I am sure that he made small talk with people. That is just part of life. Life is made up of the simple and the profound. In order to have strong relationships, we need to be able to talk to people even when they are in the flesh. Sadly, many people don't know how to properly engage with others socially.

11 - Confusing Conversations

"Dear Matthew, Are you ever irritated when people wander off topic in a conversation/argument/debate and then want to merge a lot of subjects into one when none of them go together?"

I personally had a friend in the past. I felt led to him and believed that Jesus wanted to tell him something. When I would bring up a specific topic, he would change the subject and wouldn't let me say what I was going to say.

I'd listen to him respectfully and finish that conversation. Twenty minutes later, I'd start to direct the subject back to what I wanted to say, and off he'd go again on another rabbit trail. I finally had to tell him, "I've been trying to tell you something for two hours now, but every time I start to talk, you change the subject. I want you to shut your mouth now, and I'm going to tell you what God wants you to know."

I finally recognized that he had a Jezebel spirit. The Jezebel spirit was a witchcraft spirit and could tell what God wanted to say to him and could read my mind. The spirit could tell in advance that I was just about to say something that would bring change to his life and that would confront and convict him of something.

The problem with people rambling about all these topics that don't relate to each other seems to be spiritual. I would tell them, "You're dealing with something spiritual, a spiritual entity." This spiritual entity causes people to wander, go off topic and change the subject because what you're talking about is uncomfortable to them. They'd prefer to start a conversation about 10 different subjects because they're actually nervous. They don't actually want to speak about what you're talking about, so they'll talk about anything else in order to fill in the space.

They are directed by a spirit in them so that they change the subject. I regularly find this with the church. The church is busy having services each week, but when is the last time that you've heard a pastor talk about being set apart, being holy and not serving the lust of the world? When have you heard the pastor address coming out of the world and living for God and not living according to the flesh? When have you heard a pastor speak about the commands of Jesus? When have you heard a pastor say that Jesus had 50 commands and that we should obey them and pursue them and practice them as Christians?

The church seems to have an overriding spirit that keeps pastors from teaching on the very essentials and the meat of the Word. Instead, they seem to teach on the milk of the Word every week.

Personally, I don't really have to go to a church to grow in my faith and sustain me because I'm learning from God all the time. God is always giving me revelations and wisdom, and I tend to find it quite boring to listen to a sermon. Many times, I really have to still myself and purposely engage in listening to a sermon because most of what the pastor has to say is really baby food to me.

I understand that you can start a conversation or a debate with a person. Some people like to debate or argue. They like to have heated conversations on Facebook. However, I've only ever seen someone's mind changed once on a Facebook thread. Most of the time, these people argue for the sake of arguing.

If people like going off topic and changing the subject, I would tend to think that the person likely had a Jezebel spirit that intentionally changed the topic when the Holy Spirit wanted to tell him something.

I am persuaded by God in many of my books to teach people to come out of the world and to obey the commands of Jesus Christ. Jesus keeps returning me to those subjects.

The Holy Spirit keeps on directing me to speak about those topics because they're so important to the Holy Spirit. He wants people to focus on living the way that Jesus taught. This subject has been neglected in church. However, even though people can change the subject if they talk to you, they can't change the subject in a book. They can either skip over that chapter in the book, or they can read it. They can't ignore it. Jesus is always persuading me to speak about this subject, so I would personally say that these influencing spirits are affecting your friends and the people you're talking to. This allows them to find a reason to change the subject.

You have to focus on avoiding the topic to talk about 10 subjects that don't have much to do with each other. You are dealing with a lot of distraction and dealing with something spiritual.

Some people might think that I am too concerned about Jezebel because I mentioned her twice so far in this book. They might think that I'm overly spiritual. They are right. I do live in a spiritual world, and I see much more spiritually than the average Christian sees. I experience a lot more than the average Christian experiences. You will find that if you pursue becoming a prophet, this world is more spiritual than it is fleshly. When you really tap into the spiritual realm, you will realize a lot more is happening than you can imagine.

12 - Symbolism

"Dear Matthew, What's the meaning or symbolism of colors, animals, numbers and other items? Why do certain objects, such as butterflies or dragonflies, keep reappearing?"

Many people who are called to be prophetic are called to be seers, and the loose definition of a seer is someone who sees things like visions, dreams and symbols. These objects actually mean a lot more to a person. When I prophesy, I sometimes see a vision or a picture in my mind, and I describe the picture, which has a meaning for the prophecy. The image actually gives the prophecy more meaning than just actual words.

My favorite color is blue, sky blue, to be exact. Jesus also really likes sky blue. When women wear blue, it positively affects me. Likewise, the eagle is a symbolic sign of the prophetic as is the owl, so seeing a picture of an eagle resonates with me and gives me a sort of spiritual high, making me feel a special way. Seeing an owl, which is also prophetic, touches me and affects me in a certain way as well. I'm really attracted to cats, so they also affect me, but I'm not really affected by symbolism.

However, I understand that you might be, and different people are affected in different ways by something that comes up in their visions or dreams. For example, you might have a favorite color that appears as a filter over your dream, or you might see people in that color or see that color a lot in your dream. This affects you prophetically and allows a gate to open that starts a prophetic flow that manifests in your life. When you commented on seeing lots of butterflies or dragonflies, butterflies always touch me, but I haven't ever seen a lot of them together. I've only ever seen one of them. Dragonflies are mysterious; I haven't seen many of them in my life, but they're interesting creatures. If I saw a whole lot of dragonflies or butterflies, I would also wonder what that meant. I can imagine seeing these insects would affect you. A lot of people think that dragonflies and butterflies symbolize God moving or even good luck. That makes sense to me. Butterflies are beautiful creatures.

If symbolism, certain colors, animals or certain objects cross your path, and they make you feel a certain way, tune into that. Ask God why those objects are making you feel that way. Expect those things to influence your life and expect to move with that influence and to be affected accordingly. Allow God to speak to you and use the different symbols in your life to affect you however he wants to affect you. Jesus and God are very spiritual people; they operate on another level. As you pursue your relationship as a prophet, as you grow in your prophetic understanding and you grow in your relationship with God, God will use various elements and objects to speak to you and touch you.

My former wife's name was Sharryn, so the name 'Sharon' affects me. Certain names will affect you positively if you had a strong relationship with the person and hear the same name again. You will love that name and the feeling that the name gives you. So be aware that God is going to speak to you in various ways. Be open to what he has to say and what he is speaking through the various symbols that you come across.

Symbolism and symbols are very important to people who interpret dreams. Seers understand symbols and are more affected by symbols than I am. I see in the Spirit very well, and I can communicate with angels, speak to angels and write books about them. I can also speak to saints and interact with them. I can go to heaven and interact with the people there, so I'm very spiritual with a highly active seer dimension to my life. However, I'm not as affected by symbols as you might have hoped I would be.

13 - Hearing God

"Dear Matthew, Have you ever second guessed if you were really hearing God? What if the voice sounds like your own voice, but it wasn't your own thought?"

I have to laugh at that question because all the thoughts that you have, whether they're yours or God speaking or satan speaking, are all spoken in the same tone as your thoughts. When you're starting to discern God's voice, you need to learn to recognize that the actual communication that you hear didn't originate with you.

You have to be able to recognize how your own mind thinks when a thought comes that's contrary to your own thinking. This type of recognition takes practice. For example, let us consider someone who's a good archer who shoots at targets. They don't start off shooting five arrows and making five bullseyes.

They start off like anyone else. They hit the target at the edges or completely miss it. Later, they might hit 1 in 5 bullseyes and eventually, improve until they hit 5 out of 5 bullseyes when they excel at the sport. They become proficient at shooting bullseyes by many, many hours of practice.

The same is true as you learn to speak to God and hear him speak to you. The experience comes from much practice. A good way to learn to hear God or Jesus speak is to ask them questions. Focus on God or Jesus, and by asking questions, you will learn to hear their voice.

As soon as you ask the question, the answer will start coming to you, sometimes before you even finish the question. You might say that you are just answering your own questions. You might think that you are asking a question and answering it yourself. However, if you're focusing on Jesus and you ask him a question, it actually came from Jesus. In this way, you can start to practice hearing him and getting used to his voice.

If you have three children, you will learn to recognize each of their voices. When a voice comes up behind you, you know which child is talking without turning around. The same is true with the voice of God, the voice of Jesus and the voice of the Holy Spirit.

You can learn to discern which voice is speaking. I have even learned how to discern the voices of the saints. Not only do God, the Holy Spirit and Jesus speak to me, but various saints from heaven speak to me as well. When I hear their voice, I recognize who actually said what and what they said since one of my gifts is discernment.

I've had a lot of practice discerning voices. Understandably, you might second guess God. You might easily think that you heard your own thoughts or thought your own thought and that it wasn't God speaking to you.

You can learn to practice by having conversations with God, asking him questions and then having conversations with him like talking with a close friend. You say something, then they reply. When you get used to having two-way conversations with God, you'll start to learn to hear and recognize his voice.

The more you practice, the more skilled you become, just like the example of the archer. Anyone can use a bow and arrow and shoot toward the target, but not everyone can actually hit 10 bullseyes in a row or achieve the level of an Olympic athlete. Anyone can hear and recognize the voice of God. It takes real skill and more practice to be able to hear God, the Holy Spirit and Jesus and to be able to discern those three voices and to be able to discern different saints from heaven speaking to you.

I have developed my ability to hear from God through a lot of practice and a lot of discerning. God might sound like your own voice, and you've got to slowly learn what he sounds like, but I can understand how you might second guess what God says. That will continue until you become well practiced at hearing him.

Of course, it's in the enemy's best interest to make you second guess God. He wants you to think that you thought up something yourself when God actually spoke to you. He would be really happy if God told you to do something and you second guessed it and decided not to do it.

The enemy is the first to jump in line and make you doubt that you actually heard from God, especially when you learn to prophesy. The enemy will tell you many times that God wasn't speaking and that you were just making up what you heard. Unless you receive really solid feedback from people that you prophesy to, you might doubt that God actually spoke to you and prophesied through you.

I have had 20 years to practice prophesying and to become very skilled at it. However, if a person doesn't give me feedback, I still worry that I missed it or didn't hear everything correctly. "Hearing God's Voice Made Simple" by Praying Medic provides great information on how to hear God and how to learn to listen to him speak. You can check out his book for more on the subject.

14 - Frustrations

"Dear Matthew, Have you ever felt like no one understands your frustrations, and even if you explained them, others still wouldn't understand you?"

Have I ever felt that way? Yes, I have. Like I shared in a previous chapter, I think one of the most important things for people to understand is how to hear God's voice. However, many Christians can't hear God speak. I wish that people understood how important it is to listen to him, but many aren't interested. Instead, they want to just get by in the Christian life without hearing from God.

Another thing that I feel is very important for people to understand is the 50 commandments of Jesus and to know what they are and to learn to practice them. However, the majority of Christians have never heard of 50 commands of Jesus, and they don't even know that Jesus had 50 commands. Even when you tell them about the 50 commands, they don't do the research or put them in practice.

People also need to come out of the world and not live according to the lust of the world as 1 John 2:15 states. However, people don't know how to come out of the world. They don't know how to live a life outside of the world, and they don't know to walk with God or even know how to live with him.

They are just interested in Sunday Christianity and the life at church. As I said before, they like to carry God around like a handbag, like an accessory they use when it's convenient for them. They put him down and leave him in a certain place until they're ready to pick him up again. They certainly don't take God's presence with them everywhere they go.

They certainly don't know the commands of Jesus and practice them. The world calls them hypocrites—people who preach one thing and do another. Sadly, this is true of many Christians.

With what I've just said then, I can better answer your question: "Have you ever felt that no one understands your frustrations, and even if you explained them, others still don't understand you?" I realize that I'm talking to a higher level of people here. I recognize that if you're called to be a prophet and if you're reading this book, then you're called to a higher level of understanding and a more serious walk of faith with God. I understand that many of you would identify with these questions and with the frustrations that Katrina has, so this book will come in handy.

I realize that, you, the readers, might understand most of what I've said, but the fact is that the average

Christian doesn't comprehend these things or the frustrations that we experience. I wish that every Christian could prophesy. I wish that every Christian knew how to hear God's voice and how to prophesy. I wish that every Christian would come out of the world and focus on God's Kingdom and doing the will of God for their life and living in God's purpose for their life. I wish that Christians knew what their purpose was and that they would actively pursue it. I wish that Christians knew what Jesus taught and that they obeyed the commands of Jesus.

I have many frustrations recorded in books, and I continue to teach on this subject, not only to prophets but to the average Christian. I put it out there. I don't know how many people are actually paying attention to what I say or if they actually apply my words. I do understand why you feel that no one understands your frustrations, and even if you explained yourself, others still wouldn't understand.

That's part of the life of being a prophet that you've been called to. You've been called to a higher level of intimacy with God, and with that calling, comes frustrations. These frustrations are what prophets would call a burden—a spiritual weight that comes upon your life. God has placed these burdens on your heart to worry about and to concern you.

You should be encouraged to teach on these subjects and to share them with people so that they will live a better life. They can be frustrations or they can motivate you to teach people.

If I were you, Katrina, I would read my book on how to write a self-published Christian, non-fiction book. I would find that book, read it and learn how to write. If I were you, I would start to share your heart and teach people what is important to you.

Before you attempt a book, you might start by blogging. You can blog about topics that you want to teach on and then share your blog with people on Facebook. In any case, I encourage you to start to teach people and put a book out there on Amazon so that total strangers can find and download your book. They will listen to you, not just because you are their friend or someone that they know. Instead, they will respect you as a prophetess. They will listen to you and do what you tell them to do. As an aside, I don't call people prophetess; I just call them a prophet.

When you write books, you might not hear from the readers. Sometimes. I hear from readers, but not always, so I was very encouraged to receive your questions. It's taken me a couple of hours to record all these audio files to answer all your questions, but I'm amazed that you came across me and asked me these questions because you certainly motivated me to put together what will become a fabulous little book for people to read. I pray that you are blessed and hope that when you listen to this that you email me to tell me what you learned from all of these recordings.

I will add here that the prophet will always experience frustrations and might not have people to share their feelings with. Part of the calling of a prophet is to see things that are wrong and see things that need to change and in some way, to be a catalyst so that change comes about. Not everyone will understand you or share your frustrations, but if you can use your frustrations to propel you into helping people make a change, then that will be worthwhile.

Closing Thoughts

You might have read this short book and wondered why you ever wanted to be a prophet. No one chooses the call of prophet for their life. God calls you and like Jonah, you can run from the calling.

I love who I am. Even though this life is sad sometimes and although I am lonely, and I struggle sometimes, I receive a lot of joy from publishing books and speaking into the lives of many people.

This book developed when one person asked me questions about my experiences as a prophet. It took some time, some effort and some money to write. Greg and Jeannie contributed to the expenses related to the writing and publishing of this book.

I have a big heart for prophets. We tend to fly at higher heights, and we tend to plunge to deeper depths—we really are the "deep calling unto deep." I pray that this book has blessed you and that you have learned a few things from my journey and from what I have written.

The calling of a prophet can be tough, but when rewards are given out in heaven, prophets who have done their job will receive special honor. I welcome you to the tribes of prophets who will march across this world in the last days.

I'd love to hear from you

One of the ways that you can bless me as a writer is by writing an honest and candid review of my book on Amazon. I always read the reviews of my books, and I would love to hear what you have to say about this one.

Before I buy a book, I read the reviews first. You can make an informed decision about a book when you have read enough honest reviews from readers. One way to help me sell this book and to give me positive feedback is by writing a review for me. It doesn't cost you a thing but helps me and the future readers of this book enormously.

If you would like to sow money into my book writing ministry like Greg and Jeanne did when they financed this book, or if you would like to sow money into a portion of a book, please visit my website and ask me what projects I am working on.

To read my blog or to request a life coaching session or your own personal prophecy from God, you can also visit my website at http://personal-prophecy-today.com. All of your gifts will go toward the books that I write and self-publish.

To write to me about this book or to share any other thoughts with me, please feel free to contact me at my personal email address at

survivors.sanctuary@gmail.com.

You can also friend request me on Facebook at Matthew Robert Payne. Please send me a message if we have no friends in common as a lot of scammers now send me friend requests.

You can also do me a huge favor and share this book on Facebook as a recommended book to read. This will help me and other readers.

Other Books by Matthew Robert Payne

The Parables of Jesus Made Simple

The Prophetic Supernatural Experience

Prophetic Evangelism Made Simple

Your Identity in Christ

His Redeeming Love- A Memoir

Writing and Self-Publishing Christian Nonfiction

Coping with your Pain and Suffering

Living for Eternity

Jesus Speaking Today

Great Cloud of Witnesses Speak

My Radical Encounters with Angels

Finding Intimacy with Jesus Made Simple

My Radical Encounters with Angels- Book Two

A Beginner's Guide to the Prophetic

Michael Jackson Speaks from Heaven

7 Keys to Intimacy with Jesus

Conversations with God: Book 1

Optimistic Visions of Revelation

Conversations with God: Book 2

Finding Your Purpose in Christ

Influencing your World for Christ: Practical Everyday Evangelism

My Visits to the Galactic Council of Heaven

You can find my published books on my Amazon author page here: http://tinyurl.com/jq3h893

Upcoming Books:

The Parables of Jesus Made Simple: Updated and Expanded Edition

About the Author

Matthew was raised in a Baptist church and was led to the Lord at the tender age of 8. He has experienced some pain and darkness in his life, which has given him a deep compassion and love for all people.

Today, he runs two Facebook groups, "Open Heavens and Intimacy with Jesus" and "Prophetic Training Group." Matthew has a commission from the Lord to train up prophets and to mentor others in the Christian faith. He does this through his groups and by writing relevant books on the Christian faith.

God has commissioned him to write at least 50 books in his life, and he spends his days writing and earning the money to self-publish. You can support him by donating money at http://personal- prophecy-today.com or by requesting your own personal prophecy or life-coaching session.

It is Matthew's prayer that this book has blessed you, and he hopes it will lead you into a deeper and more intimate relationship with God.

Blurb

Open the pages of this little book to read 14 questions and their answers on the life of a prophet. Matthew developed this book after a prophetess reached out to him with these questions. As he recorded the answer to each query, he decided to collect his thoughts into a book.

Katrina sought out Matthew from a deep place within her heart to a deep place within his heart. She asked him some common questions and some other questions that aren't so common. What followed was 14 voice recordings that were eventually transcribed and made into this book for other aspiring prophets and prophetesses on their journey.

Learn more about:

- Why your friends don't take you seriously as a prophet
- Why people misunderstand you
- How you can be called as a prophet yet no one recognizes you
- How losing your friends draws you closer to God

Read about each of these topics and more. The life of a prophet can be a hard and challenging road. As you dive into this book, you will find that your journey is not unusual and that what you are experiencing is quite normal. You will find hope in these pages. Matthew felt that Katrina's call for answers might be a catalyst for you and your decision to pursue God with vigor.

Jump into the deep end—where deep really does call to deep!

Lightning Source UK Ltd.
Milton Keynes UK
UKOW03n1615280517

302174UK00003B/35/P

9 781365 852541